To
Parents

Thank you for choosing our *Early Learning Fun* as your child's learning companion.

To maximize your child's experience with *Early Learning Fun*, it is vital that you provide a supportive environment in which your child can enjoy doing the activities. Here are some suggestions for you to help your child:

- Children feel a sense of achievement when they try new things and can complete them, so help your child finish whatever tasks he or she starts. Remember to give your child support whenever necessary, but refrain from taking over the task completely.

- Take the time to work with your child. Don't rush them through the activities because children need time to feel engaged with what they are doing.

- Always give encouragement. Positive reinforcement encourages children to learn and sustains their interest in learning. Look for achievements to praise and acknowledge your child's progress whenever possible.

- Nurture your child's creativity. Encourage your child to ask questions, try different ways, and engage him or her in spin-off activities that you may come up with.

With your involvement and encouragement, we are sure that your child will find working through *Early Learning Fun* a fun and rewarding experience.

Contents

Alphabet Fun

A for alligator

alligator

Trace the letter Aa.

apple

ant

Anna

Color the paths to help the squirrel gather food items that start with Aa. Then color the food items.

peanut

acorn

apple

leaf

Bb

bird

B for bird

Trace the letter Bb.

bear

book

 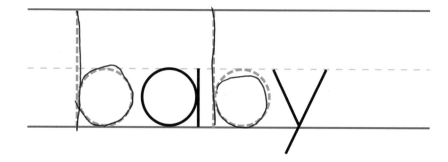

baby

Trace the letter **B** or **b** and color those balls.

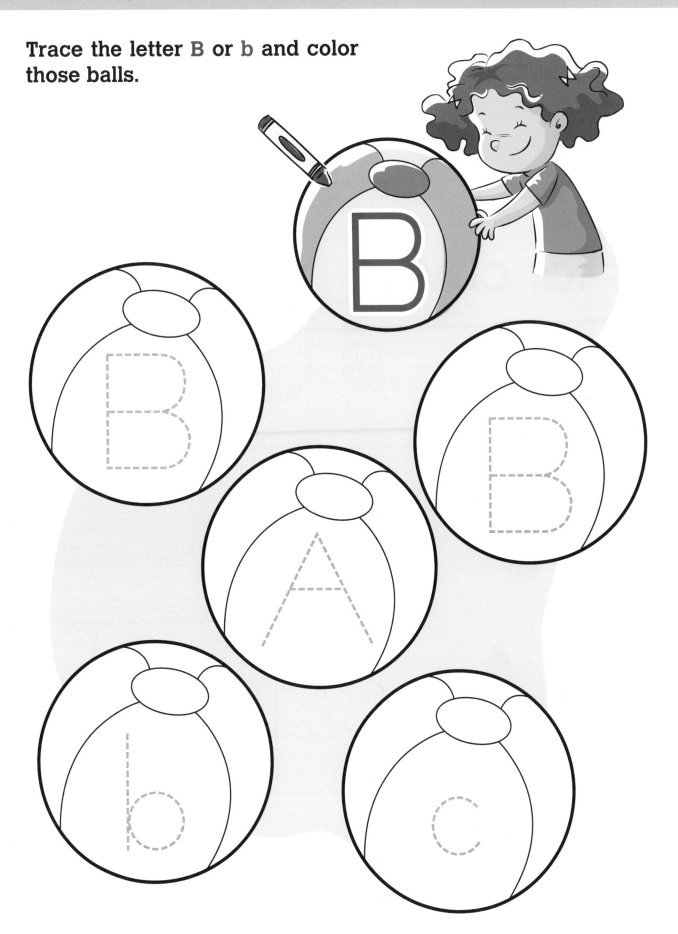

C c

C for cow

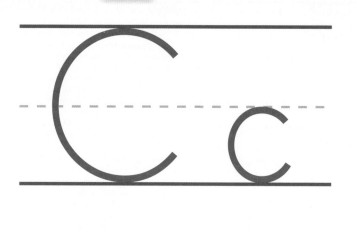

cow

Trace the letter Cc.

cat

carrot

clock

Color the hot air balloon.

C = others =   c =   others =

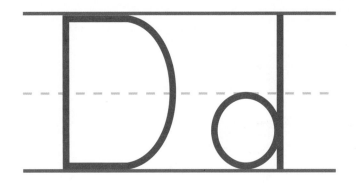

D for dolphin

dolphin

Trace the letter Dd.

dog

donkey

Daddy

Get the ducklings to their mom without going past the dogs.

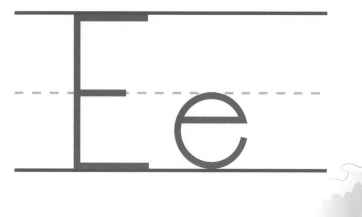

Ee

E for elephant

elephant

Trace the letter Ee.

Earth

egg

eagle

Trace the letter Ee and draw the missing eye and ear.

frog

F for frog

Trace the letter Ff.

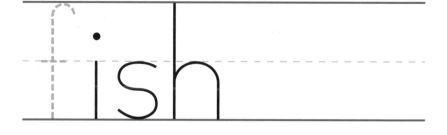

fish

flowers

farm

Trace the letter F or f and color those flowers.

G for gorilla

gorilla

Trace the letter Gg.

giraffe

Granny

goose

Trace the lines from the mother goat to the baby goats. Trace the letter **Gg**.

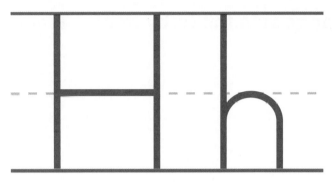

H for hippo

hippo

Trace the letter Hh.

Trace the letter Hh and print the missing one.

Find and circle A, B, C, D, E, F, G, and H.

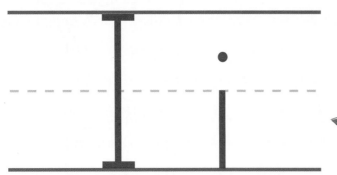

I for iguana

Trace the letter Ii.

Color the snail. Then trace the letter Ii.

I =   i =   others =

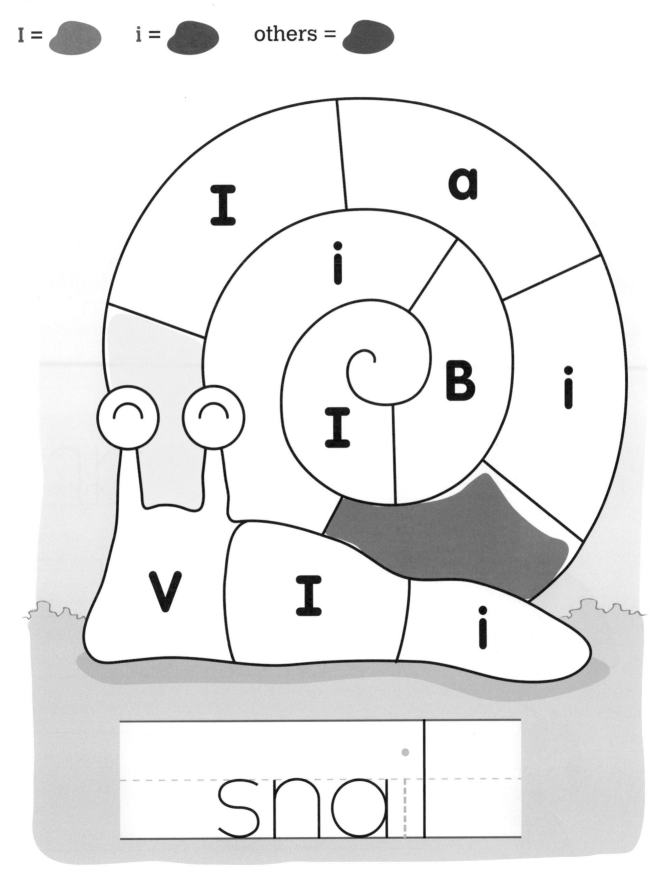

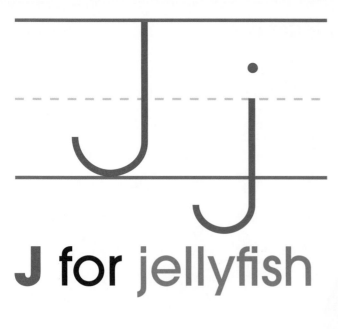

J for jellyfish

jellyfish

Trace the letter Jj.

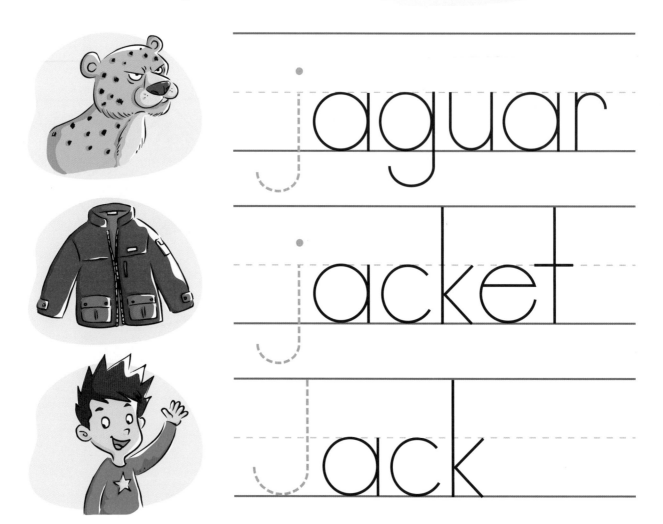

jaguar

jacket

Jack

Draw lines to give the items that start with Jj to the jellyfish.

jar

fish

juice

pencil

lollipop

jelly beans

seashell

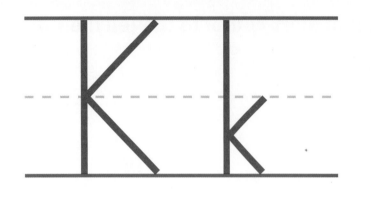

kangaroo

K for kangaroo

Trace the letter Kk.

koala

key

kite

Trace only the signs that have the letter K or k to take the dog to the boy.

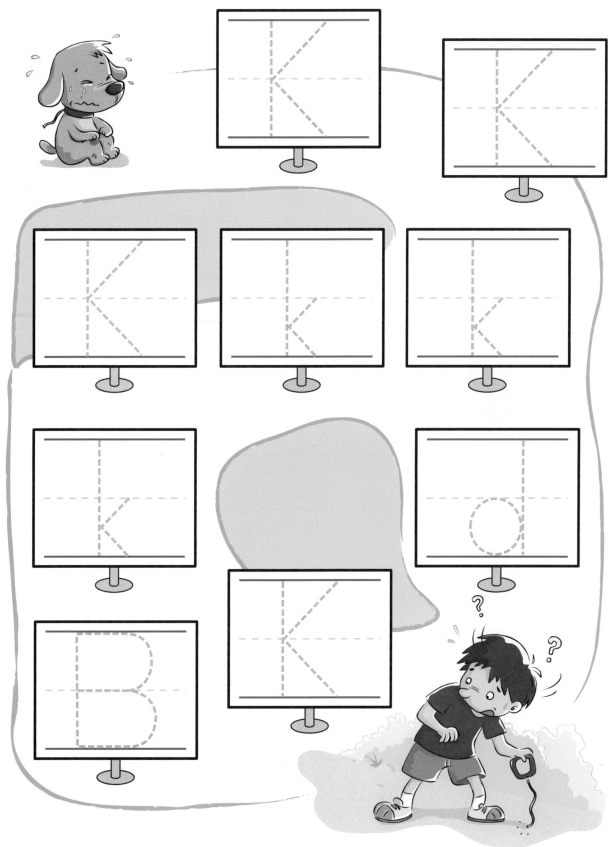

L for lion

Trace the letter Ll.

oon

eaf

ama

Find the ice cubes shaped like L or l in the lemonade. Trace and color them.

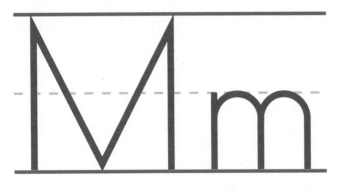

M for moose

moose

Trace the letter Mm.

moon

monkey

Mom

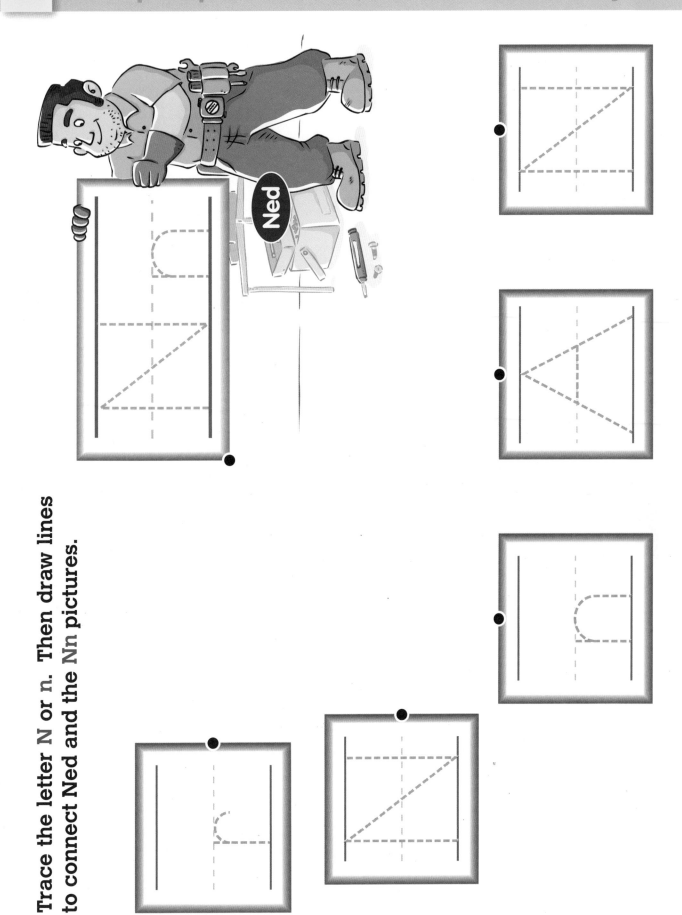

Trace the letter N or n. Then draw lines to connect Ned and the Nn pictures.

Ned

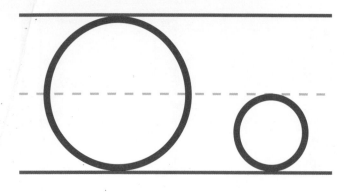

ostrich

O for ostrich

Trace the letter Oo.

otter

orange

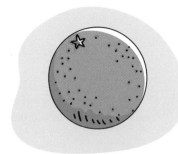

octopus

Trace the letter Oo. Then trace the lines to connect the cards with the correct pictures.

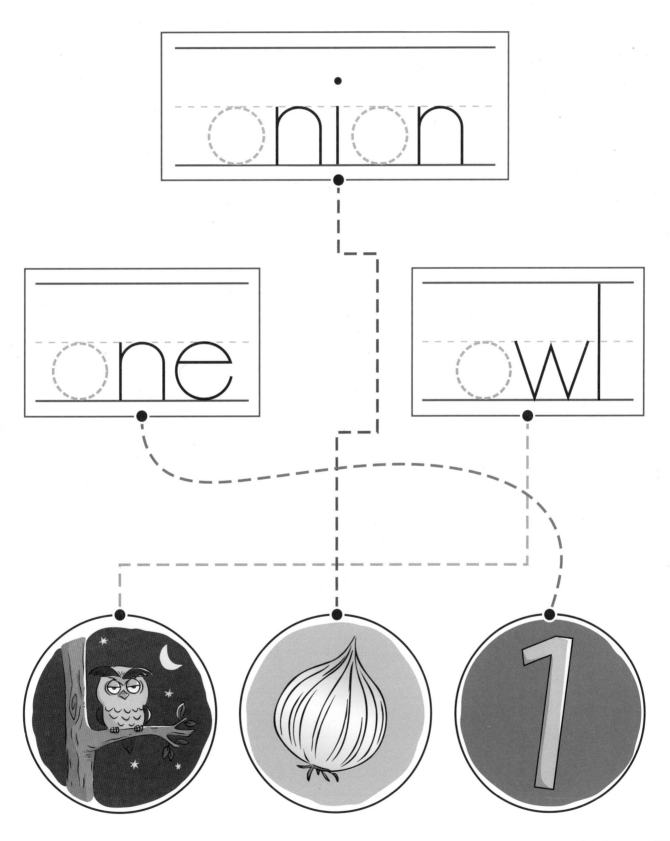

Aa Bb Cc Dd Ee Ff Gg Hh Ii Jj Kk Ll Mm

Pp

P for penguin

penguin

Trace the letter Pp.

pig

parrot

panda

Trace the letter Pp. Then circle the objects that match the words.

pen

pizza

pumpkin

quail

Q for quail

Trace the letter Qq.

quarter

queen

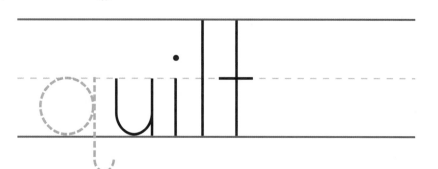

quilt

Help the queen choose the crowns that have the letter Q or q by coloring them. Then print the missing letter.

_____ueen

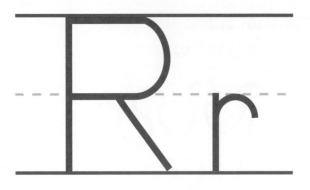

rhino

R for rhino

Trace the letter Rr.

rabbit

rose

rooster

Help the rabbits collect the raindrops that have the letter R or r by coloring them.

S s

S for snake

snake

Trace the letter Ss.

seat

swan

Santa

Draw lines to connect the spider with the
things that start with Ss.

spider

sun

sunglasses

scissors

book

cup

saw

grass

strawberry

T for tiger

Trace the letter Tt.

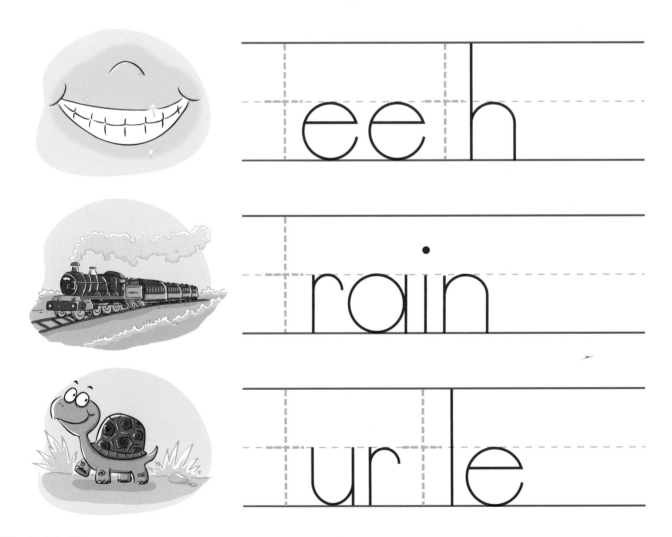

Color the tree.

T = t = others =

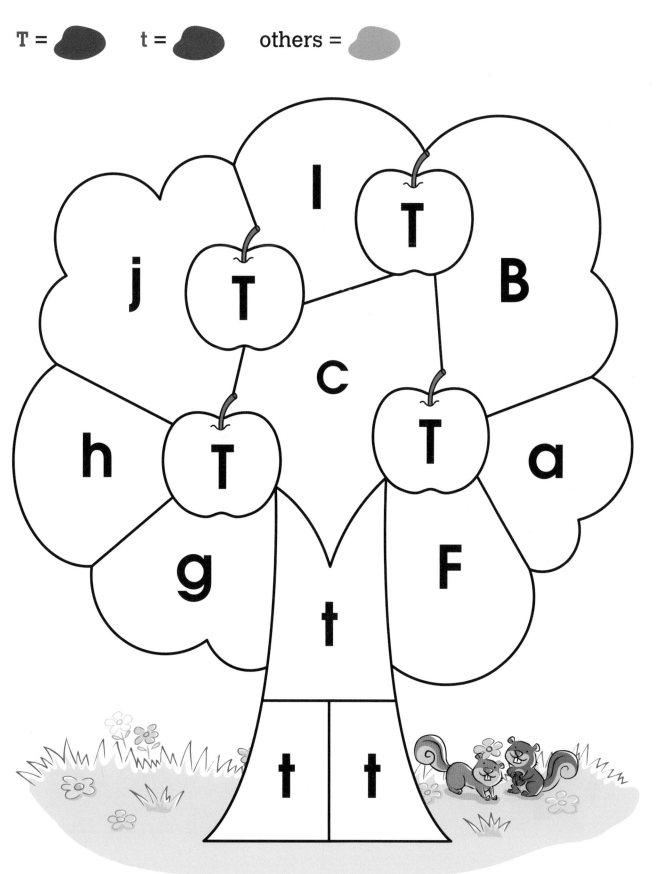

Uu

U for unicorn

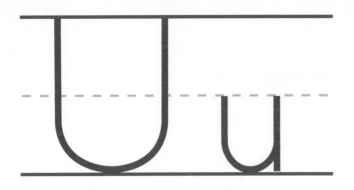

unicorn

Trace the letter Uu.

uncle

umpire

up

Print the letter u to complete the word. Then color the umbrellas that have the letter U or u.

mbrella

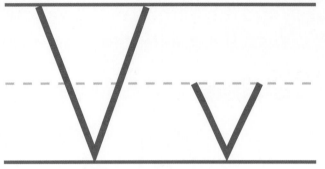

V for vulture

vulture

Trace the letter Vv.

 vase

 vacuum

 van

Print the letter V in the green boxes and the letter v in the yellow boxes to complete the words. Then do the matching.

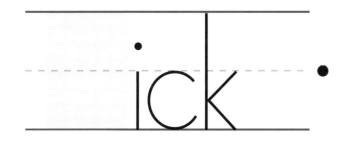 • ick

 • **hive**

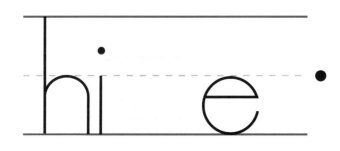 hi_e •

 • **Vick**

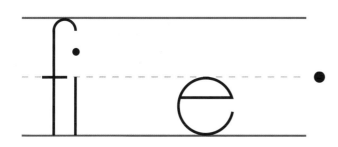 fi_e •

 • **Val**

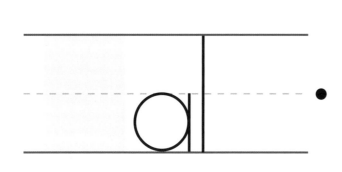 _al •

 • **5** five

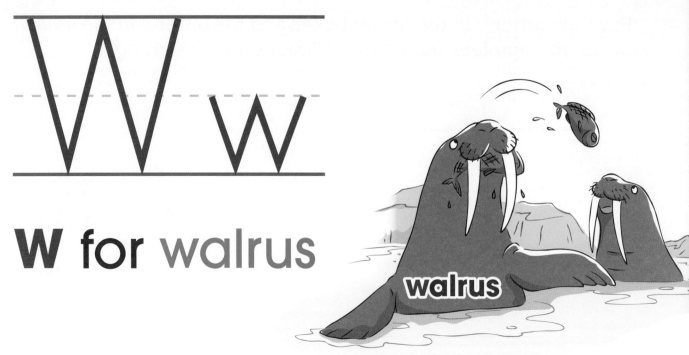

W for walrus

walrus

Trace the letter Ww.

wolf

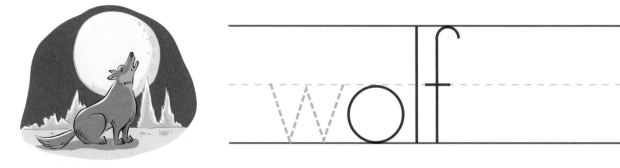

wizard

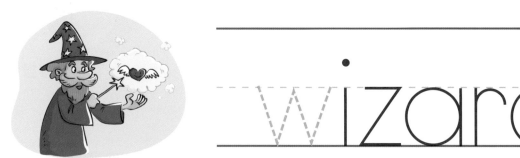

worm

Trace the missing parts to complete the letter Ww. Then trace the letter w to complete the word.

X for X-ray fish

Trace the letter Xx.

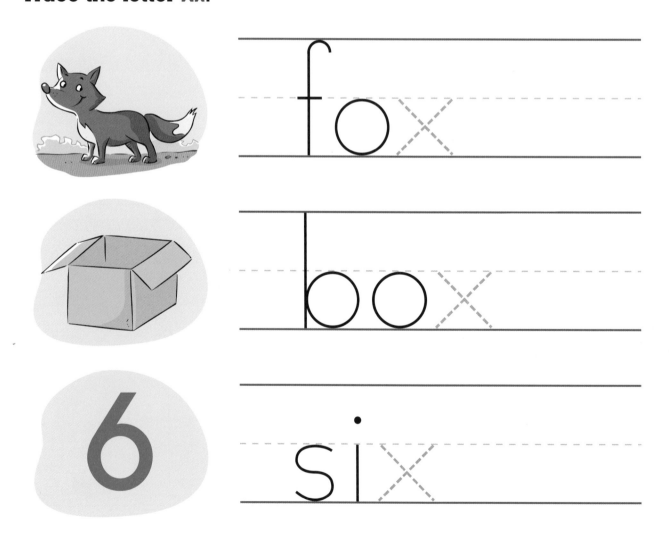

Print the missing letter. Then color the xylophone.

x =
x =
others =

y_lophone

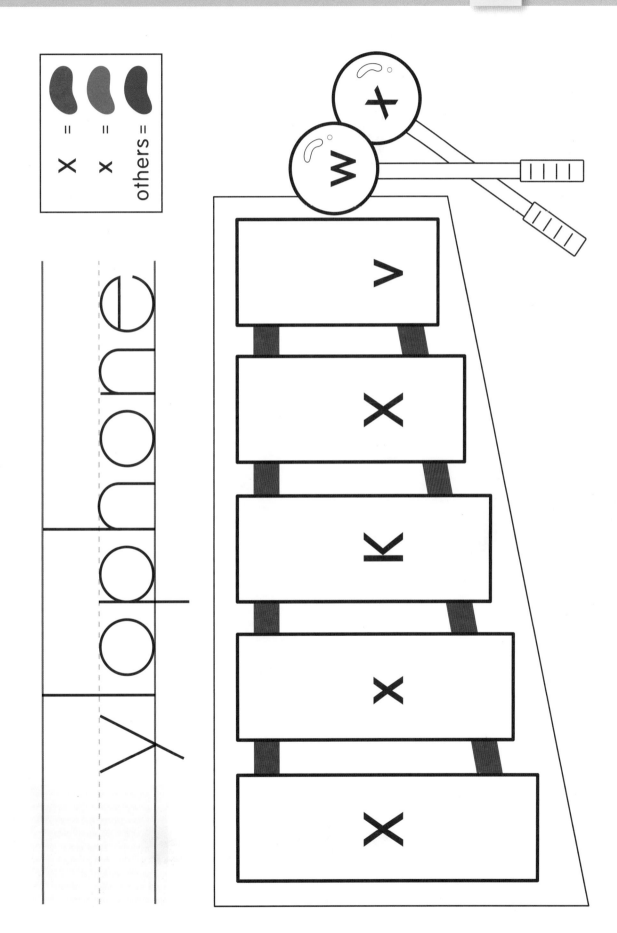

Aa Bb Cc Dd Ee Ff Gg Hh Ii Jj Kk Ll Mm

Y for yak

Trace the letter Yy.

yacht

yoga

yo-yo

Trace the letter Yy. Then color the yo-yo yellow.

Zz

zebra

Z for zebra

Trace the letter Zz.

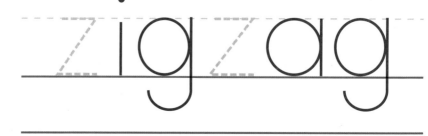

zigzag

zipper

zoo

Print a Z on the zebras. Then lead the zebras to the pen by coloring their zigzag paths.

Zebra
Pen

Aa to Zz

Color the boxes from A to Z to help the children get to school.

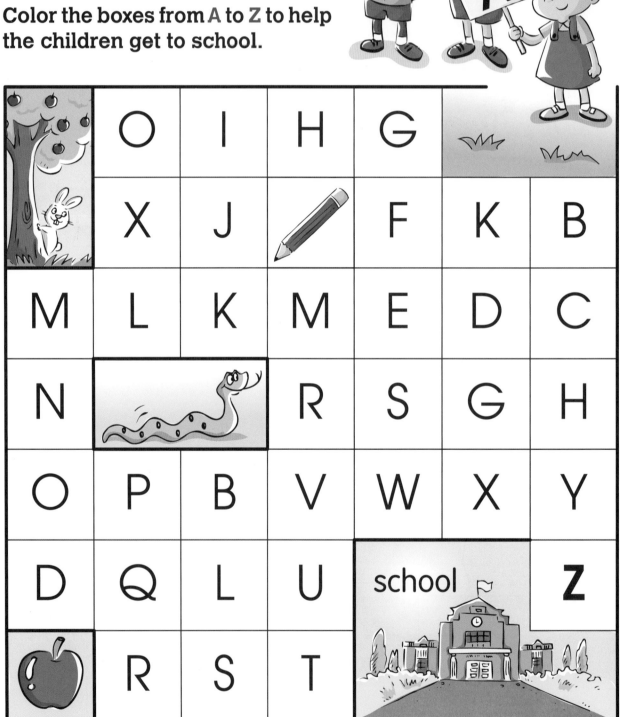

	O	I	H	G	
	X	J	✏️	F	K	B
M	L	K	M	E	D	C
N	🐛		R	S	G	H
O	P	B	V	W	X	Y
D	Q	L	U	school		Z
🍎	R	S	T		

Connect the letters from a to z. Print the missing letters.

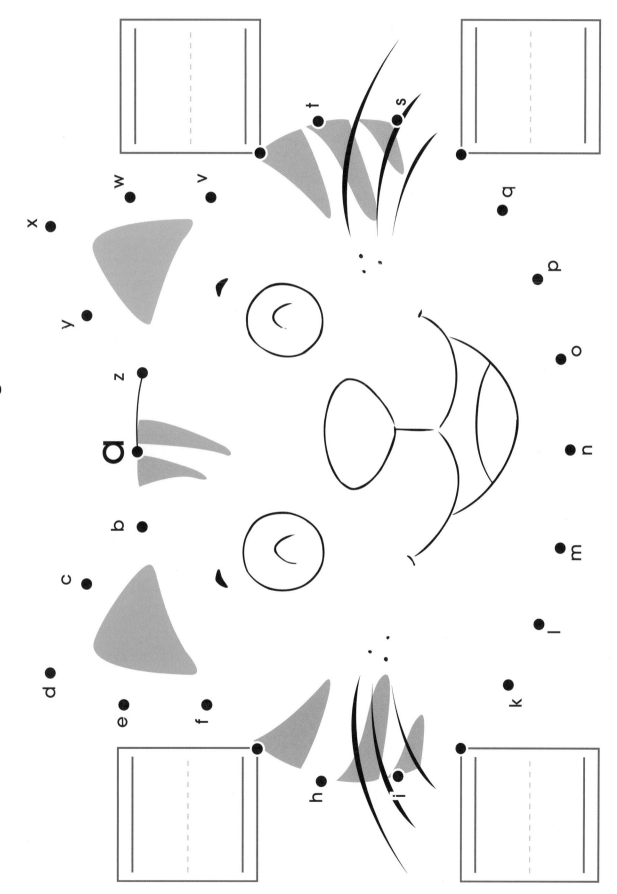